FAKE
YOUR OWN
ANTIQUES

FAKE
YOUR OWN
ANTIQUES

PETER KNOTT

NORTH LIGHT BOOKS

Cincinnati, Ohio

First published in North America
in 1996 by North Light Books,
an imprint of F&W Publications, Inc.,
1507 Dana Avenue, Cincinnati, OH 45207
1-800/289-0963

ISBN 0-89134-765-8

This book was designed and produced by
Quarto Publishing plc
The Old Brewery
6 Blundell Street
London N7 9BH

Editor Cathy Marriott
Senior Art Editor Antonio Toma
Copy Editor Chester Krone
Designer Roger Daniels
Photographers Ian Howes, Paul Forrester
Editorial Director Mark Dartford
Art Director Moira Clinch

Typeset by Type Technique, London W1
Manufactured by Eray Scan Pte Ltd, Singapore
Printed by Leefung-Asco Printers Ltd, China

CONTENTS

❖

WOOD

Metal

Paper and Leather

Plaster and Stone

GLASS AND CERAMIC

PLASTIC

COMPOSITION BOARD

INTRODUCTION

❖

This book is designed to help you recreate the natural style and beauty of original and antique fixtures and fittings. It is possible to imitate the natural aging process in a fraction of the time – and also have fun in the process!

Have you ever thought how nice it would be to have your very own antiques and period pieces which

also blend with your decor? This book will help you develop your craft skills while you create a variety of different antique finishes. Projects can be easily adapted and coordinated to blend with your existing decor because you have infinite flexibility in choice of design, color and texture. Most finishes can be adapted very easily, so consider the projects as typical examples, which will hopefully inspire you to create a wonderful array of decorative items.

Forty projects are demonstrated, showing methods of making surfaces look as if they have aged well. For example, you can treat photocopies to produce aged prints, distress new wood to give it the patina of antiquity, and transform pedestrian plastic into majestic marble. The book is divided into sections by material and examines different ways of treating each surface, including wood, ceramic, leather, glass, metal, paper, plastic and plaster. Each project is illustrated with step-by-step instructions for every stage of the process, be it painting, staining, stencilling, distressing, stripping, varnishing or weathering.

Most surfaces undergo considerable change over a period of time, and these effects can be faithfully imitated to create the impression of these changes. Sometimes it is possible to accelerate the natural process, such as the aging of new stone. At other times, aging can be imitated using a variety of techniques. The projects demonstrated will allow you to master finishes such as decoupage, verdigris, craqueleure and metal patina to create the style and character of a bygone age.

We have used a combination of new and junk shop items to illustrate appropriate techniques for a range of surfaces.

Each chapter illustrates typical techniques which can be used on a particular surface and often suggests suitable methods for completely changing the appearance of the surface, such as giving plastic the appearance of stone or transforming wood to look like leather. Most techniques can be adapted for a variety of materials, and each project should be regarded as a starting point to let your imagination run wild. Don't be afraid to experiment and adapt techniques. It is part of the fun with decorative finishes that each time you play you will create an original look and style. The possibilities are endless – you could marble- or stone-finish that plain laminate table that you found in a junk shop or create your own stained glass window. Try it and be prepared to have as much fun as I did in preparing this book for you.

TOOLS

❖

You probably already possess some of the basic equipment needed to create your own antiques. However, it is inevitable that you may require some specialist tools and materials to complete some projects. Most tools are readily available from local hardware stores or craft suppliers. Always work on a clean, flat surface and keep sharp implements beyond the reach of children. For best results use the paintbrush recommended for the type of paint that you are using. Use a fine paintbrush for detailed work and a stencil brush for stencilling. Always clean brushes and tools well immediately after use.

Steel w

Metal brush

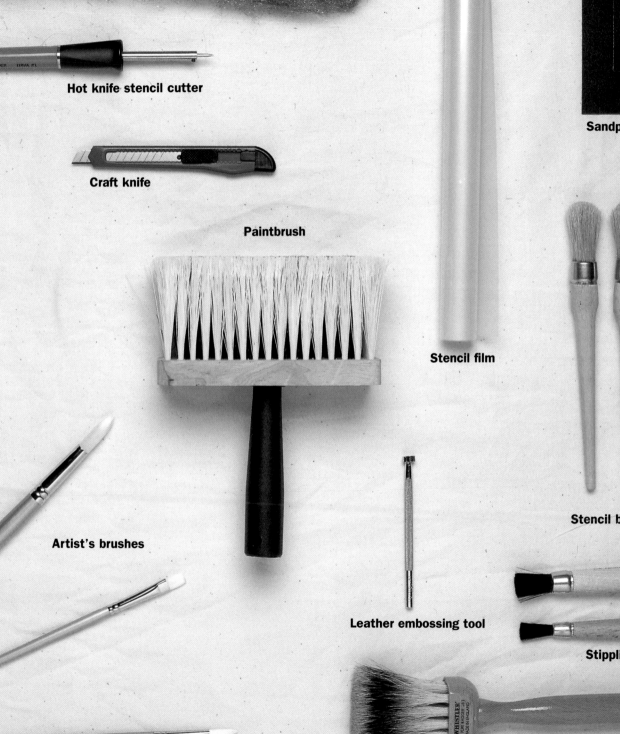

Hot knife stencil cutter

Craft knife

Paintbrush

Sandpaper

Stencil film

Stencil brushes

Artist's brushes

Leather embossing tool

Stippling brushes

Softening brush

MATERIALS

❖

It is essential that the appropriate material is used for a particular job. There is no point in using a paint which will wash off the surface the first time it is cleaned. Fortunately, a wide choice of products is available, allowing you to achieve the best possible results in the easiest and safest way. It is advisable to protect most finished items with varnish. Remember to varnish in a dust-free area. Oil paints are useful for specialized paint techniques. Although they are slow-drying, the results are worth waiting for. Spray paints are good for giving an even covering of paint. Always spray in a well-ventilated room and place the item in a large cardboard box to protect the surrounding area. Use sprays that are free from harmful CFCs. Take care when using materials containing solvents and other toxic substances. Always follow the manufacturer's instructions and take note of safety recommendations.

Caustic soda

Varnish

Scumble glaze

Stencil paint

Metal powders

Two-pack craqueleure

Artist's oil paint

Patina varnish

Gum arabic

Spray paint

Decoupage paper scraps

Rubber cement

Ammonia

Cold cure ceramic paint

Craft glue

Denatured alcohol

AMMONIA SOLUTION

Paint remover

Metal patinating solutions

Furniture wax

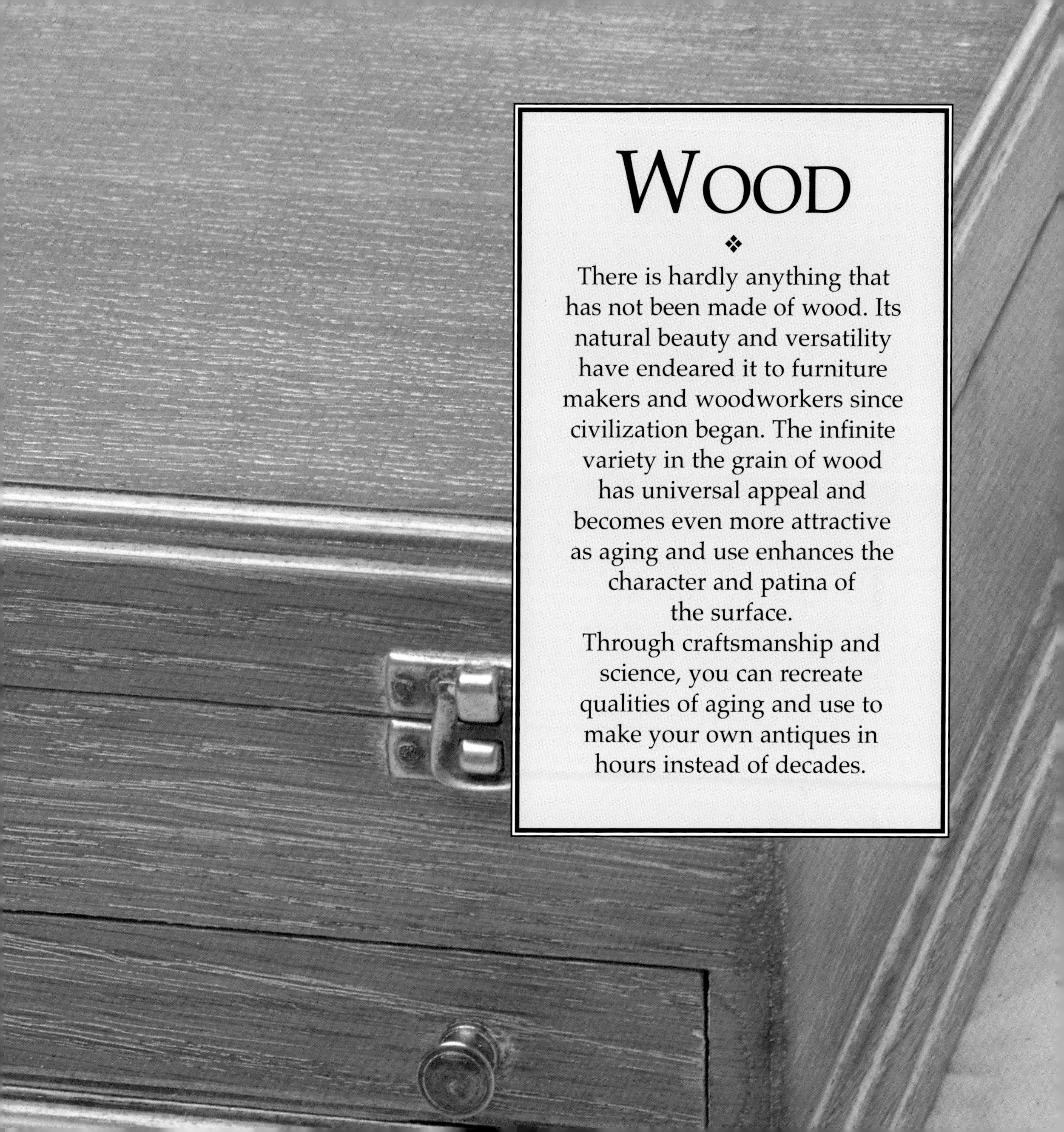

WOOD

❖

There is hardly anything that
has not been made of wood. Its
natural beauty and versatility
have endeared it to furniture
makers and woodworkers since
civilization began. The infinite
variety in the grain of wood
has universal appeal and
becomes even more attractive
as aging and use enhances the
character and patina of
the surface.

Through craftsmanship and
science, you can recreate
qualities of aging and use to
make your own antiques in
hours instead of decades.

Aged Modern *Chest*

❖

New products like this wooden chest are now very popular and readily available. A natural look of age and patina can be achieved by applying stains, waxes and varnish to almost any wooden surface.

❖

You will need...
- Dark oak solvent stain
- Soft cloth
- Acrylic- or oil-based varnish
- Varnish brush
- Sandpaper
- Tinted furniture wax
- Burnt umber artist's oil paint
- Steel wool

1 Apply dark oak stain with a cloth in the direction of the grain. Do not remove knobs or handles, as the natural wear and tear which you wish to imitate occurs in these areas.

2 When the stain has thoroughly dried, apply at least one coat of varnish to seal the surface. Rub lightly between coats with sandpaper.

3 Improve the quality and patina by adding layers of tinted furniture wax. Mix a little burnt umber artist's oil paint with the wax as you apply it with some steel wool.

4 Wear and tear are obvious on original pieces. To imitate this, add an extra bit of color where this would occur, such as around the drawer knobs. Buff the hardened wax to a natural finish.

Distressed
Plant
Stand

❖

Over a period of time, a piece of furniture
may be repainted many times. Because of
natural wear and tear, the layers of paint are
worn away to expose those from a previous
time. This technique shows how to imitate a
natural aged look.

❖

You will need…
- Latex paint (at least two different colors)
- Paintbrushes
- Vaseline
- Steel wool
- Sponge
- Acrylic- or oil-based varnish

1 Apply a coat of blue latex paint to a sanded wooden surface with a standard paintbrush. You can apply a number of contrasting colors at the same time.

2 When the base coat is dry, apply a little vaseline to areas subject to high wear. Apply a contrasting top coat of latex paint immediately, and apply more coats when the previous coat is thoroughly dry.

3 When thoroughly dry, rub down the whole surface with a medium grade steel wool. The vaseline prevents adhesion between the layers of paint and lets the top coats be easily removed.

4 Apply a wash of very dilute honey-colored latex paint over the whole surface with a sponge or brush to imitate the effect of aging varnish. When dry, apply a layer of varnish.

Pickled
Oak
Box

❖

Many hardwoods used to be treated with
lime to protect them against attack from
beetles and other destructive pests which
ravaged buildings and furniture. However,
the familiar white grain of treated wood has
become popular and can now be achieved
easily with pickling wax. This original box
to hold flatware is given a new lease on life
with this simple but effective technique.

❖

You will need…
- Paint remover
- Paintbrush
- Scraper
- Steel wool
- Soft metal brush
- Pickling wax
- Furniture wax
- Soft cloth

1 Apply paint remover to the surface with a paintbrush. Follow the manufacturer's directions. Use a scraper to remove the surface varnish. Remove any remaining varnish with steel wool dipped in paint remover.

2 Remove the paler soft grain with a soft metal brush. Brush the surface vigorously in the same direction as the grain so that the surface does not become scratched.

3 Apply an even layer of pickling wax with a medium grade steel wool. Work the wax well into the previously roughened grain. Leave the box in a cool place for at least 30 minutes.

4 Work a little clear furniture wax over the surface with steel wool. Continue to work the steel wool over the surface until the desired effect is achieved. When hardened, buff to a pleasant mid-sheen finish with a soft cloth.

Ornate
Mirror
Frame

❖

There is a treasury of unwanted or damaged goods in every attic or thrift store. This simple and inexpensive frame can be transformed by using mass-produced moldings, paints and glazes. The same techniques can be easily adapted to antique doors and armoires or even walls. Play with the glazes: their extended drying time means that colors can be blended together to create many different beautiful patterns.

❖

You will need...

- Medium-grit sandpaper
- Mineral spirits
- Assorted moldings
- Craft glue
- Cellophane tape
- Soft cloth
- Flat board and weight
- Eggshell paint
- Paintbrushes
- Transparent scumble glaze and a suitable colorant
- Jar
- Old rag

1 Rub down the surface vigorously with a medium-grit sandpaper. Use either mineral spirits or liquid detergent to clean the surface.

2 Apply the chosen moldings with craft glue when the frame is thoroughly dry. Be sure to use the appropriate glue for the material. Cellophane tape will give temporary support until the glue dries.

3 Apply moldings with care and continue to build up the design. Set aside the frame until the glue is thoroughly dry. Use a flat board and weight to hold the two surfaces tightly together.

4 When the glue has dried, apply a coat of pale cream eggshell paint with a regular paintbrush. Set the frame aside to dry. Use more coats to produce a good surface.

5 The glaze for the decorative coat is normally transparent and must be tinted to your color requirements. Squeeze some artist's oil paint into a clear jar and add mineral spirits.

6 Break up and dissolve the paint with a brush or stick. Check the base of the jar to make sure that all the lumps have dissolved.

7 Add the transparent oil glaze to the jar and mix thoroughly. The mixture should contain no more than fifteen percent solvent. Acrylic water-based scumble glazes can be used as an alternative.

8 Brush the tinted glaze onto the prepared surface, taking care that all surfaces are coated. Apply two or more colored glazes and blend together if required.

9 Remove excess glaze by drying the brush in an old but clean rag or towel. Stipple the surface with a brush.

10 Dab a soft clean cloth on the surface to remove glaze from the highlights and to create the decorative finish. When the glaze has dried, apply a protective coat of varnish.

Aged
Pine
Stool

❖

Pine benefits from the ravages of time more than any other wood. Its color mellows and the dented and bruised surface takes on a character all of its own. New untreated pine can easily be treated to achieve this look.

❖

You will need…
- A bunch of keys or heavy chain
- Brown and black latex paint
- Sponge
- Sandpaper
- Blow torch
- Acrylic- or oil-based varnish
- Paintbrush
- Furniture wax
- Steel wool
- Soft cloth

WOOD

1 Beat the surface of the wood with metal items such as a bunch of keys or a heavy chain. Then apply a dirty brown wash of very thin latex paint or strong cold tea and set aside to dry.

2 When dry, smooth the surface with medium grade sandpaper. Rub a little black latex or powdered pigment into the rough and damaged areas to help highlight them and imitate the natural buildup of dirt.

3 Use a blowtorch, hot air stripper, or any other strong heat source to scorch the surface. Rub down the surface to remove any excess black paint or burn marks.

4 Apply a coat of water-based acrylic varnish. When dry, apply a generous coat of furniture wax with steel wool and leave in a cool, dry place while the wax hardens. Polish with a soft cloth.

Restored
Toy
Box

❖

Some pieces of furniture will always find a
good home, and this wonderful chest is just
ready for restoration to give it a new lease
on life. The panels are finished with an
imitation leather while the contrasting
banding imitates iron to create the
impression of quality and strength.

❖

You will need…
- Sandpaper
- Latex paint and thickener
- Assorted brushes
- Texturing tool
- Soft rags
- Furniture wax and artist's oil paint
- Steel wool
- Mineral spirits
- Silver paint
- Black latex paint or scumble glaze
- Acrylic varnish

1 Rub down the surface with sandpaper. Thicken latex paint by mixing it with whiting, filler or a powdered texturing medium and apply. Use a stipple brush or other texturing tool to create a random swirling pattern and leave to dry.

2 Color a little furniture wax with artist's oil paint and apply to the surface with a brush or steel wool. A mixture of similar colors gives a good effect; build up multiple layers as the wax hardens.

3 Wash the banding with mineral spirits. Let it dry before applying a coat of silver paint. If cissing occurs, rewash the surface and reapply the paint.

4 When the silver paint has thoroughly hardened, wipe a wash of thinned black latex paint or black scumble glaze over the surface to create a realistic iron look. Apply varnish to protect the surface.

Mock
Bamboo
Towel Rack

❖

Bamboo was extremely popular with the
Victorians, but went out of fashion for many
years at the turn of the century. Today,
however, bamboo, both real and imitation,
is very popular. This modern reproduction
towel rack with its mock bamboo rails looks
wonderfully authentic. Anything from
banister spindles to unsightly pipes can be
treated using this technique.

❖

You will need…
- Cream, honey-colored and black
latex paint
- Sandpaper
- Paintbrushes
- Sponge
- Acrylic varnish
- Transparent scumble glaze and colorants
- Soft cloth
- Oil-based satin varnish

1 Apply a coat of cream latex paint to a prepared and sanded surface.

2 When the first coat has dried, rub down with sandpaper, clean and repaint until a good finish has been achieved. When dry, apply a thin wash of honey-colored latex paint with either a sponge or a brush.

3 Apply a coat of acrylic varnish to seal the surface and leave to dry.

4 Brush on a coat of dark brown tinted scumble glaze to each of the rails. Either acrylic- or solvent-based scumbles are suitable.

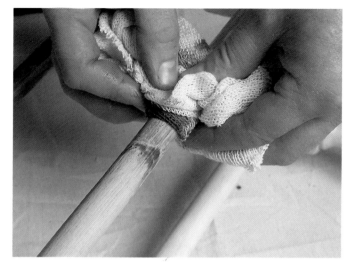

5 Use a soft cloth to form a pad around the rail and push the glaze to create rings at irregular points along the length of the rail.

6 Continue to build up the glaze. Add second and third layers if required.

7 When the surface is dry, paint on characteristic black bands to imitate bamboo with a fine brush.

8 Stipple the ends of the towel rack with a rich brown scumble glaze. When dry, apply oil-based satin varnish to protect the surface. Apply a minimum of two coats.

Wax
Distressed
Display
Cabinet

❖

Mixing materials which react with each
other can often be exploited to great effect.
One of the most obvious and easiest
examples of this is wax distressing, where a
turpentine-based furniture wax is used to
cut through the water-based latex paint and
expose some of the base color. This beautiful
new pine cabinet lends itself perfectly to
this sort of technique.

❖

You will need...
- Two contrasting latex paints
- Assorted brushes
- Water-based acrylic gold paint
- Furniture wax
- Steel wool
- Soft cloth
- Mineral spirits
- Gilding cream

1 Paint the bare pine with at least two coats of white latex paint and, when this is thoroughly dry, apply a top coat in a contrasting color.

2 When the top coat has dried, highlight the moldings with the gold paint. This dries very quickly and, to achieve a good metallic finish, add more coats.

3 Leave the paints to harden overnight and then work a little furniture wax over the surface with steel wool. Remove varying amounts of the softened top coat with steel wool if desired.

4 Leave the wax to harden and then polish to a natural sheen. Clean the glass with a cloth and mineral spirits. Use a little gilding cream to highlight the moldings.

Painted
and Stencilled
Box

❖

Stencilling is one of the easiest and most
effective paint finish techniques. You can
transform even the simplest of items into a
wonderful treasure. In recent years,
unfinished plain items, such as this simple
veneer box, have become widely available,
and are ideally suited to undergo a
transformation.

❖

You will need...
- Water-based paint
- Paintbrushes
- Sandpaper
- Stencil
- Spray adhesive/masking tape
- Stencil brushes and paint
- Palette or old plate
- Acrylic- or oil-based varnish

1 Paint the box with at least two coats of water-based paint, such as latex or acrylic. Leave sufficient drying time between coats to rub down the surface with sandpaper if required.

2 Attach the stencil with spray adhesive or masking tape. This stencil is hand-cut, but pre-cut designs are widely available. Work the stencil paint into the brush on the palette. Stipple or swirl the brush through the stencil.

3 Add second or even third coats to build up the intensity of color. Apply the paint quickly since stencil paint dries almost instantly.

4 Carefully remove the stencil to reveal your masterpiece, which can be further enhanced with more stencilling, or even a little hand-painted detail. Varnish the box for durability.

Decoupaged
and Crackled
Music Box

❖

Although the era of the phonograph is past,
we redecorated this wonderful music box to
provide an eye-catching piece of furniture
ideal for any number of uses. The original
oak had, at some time, been painted. Rather
than strip it, we decided to finish it with an
acrylic crackle and then decoupage it with
music scores to evoke its former glory.

❖

You will need...
- Medium grade sandpaper
- Two water-based paints
- Paintbrushes
- Acrylic crackle medium
- Acrylic- or oil-based varnish
- Decoupage sheets
- Craft knife/scissors
- Strong cold tea
- Craft glue

1 Rub down the surface with a medium grade sandpaper to provide a sound and good surface for subsequent coats.

2 On all surfaces which are to be crackled, apply a coat of the colored paint which will show through the cracks. Either a latex or acrylic paint is suitable.

3 When the base coat has dried, apply a coat of acrylic crackle medium. The coat's thickness determines the type of cracks which are formed, so experiment on a sample surface.

4 Leave the surface until dry and apply a top coat of a contrasting color of latex or acrylic paint. Apply once only in the same direction as the crackle medium.

5 As the top coat dries, crackling will continue and create an old, crackled paint effect. If you are not happy with the finish, seal it with varnish before starting again.

6 Trim sheets of music, photocopied from a music manuscript, to size and soak them in a strong solution of cold tea long enough to achieve the desired degree of discoloration.

7 Glue the still-damp paper to the surface with craft glue. Take care to remove trapped air, while not rubbing the soft face excessively.

8 Carefully mark and trim the paper so that it fits the panels. As the damp paper is very soft, take care to avoid tearing it. Continue to apply sheets, overlapping as required. Leave to dry thoroughly.

Early American Kitchen Towel Rack

❖

The early American settlers very quickly established a unique design look which often combined German, Dutch and native American influences. To create the natural Shaker style, they made paints from assorted mixtures of lime, pigment and egg white, and decorated the painted objects with naive or folk-style hand painting or stencilling. This kitchen towel rack recreates this popular look using modern milk or Shaker paints.

❖

You will need...
- Sandpaper
- Shaker or milk paint
- Paintbrush
- Stencil
- Spray adhesive/masking tape
- Stencil paint and brushes
- Acrylic- or oil-based varnish

1 Rub down the lacquered surface of the towel rack with sandpaper. Mix the milk or Shaker paints with water just before use. Always follow the directions since the paint is alkaline and can cause burning.

3 When dry, attach the stencil with spray adhesive or masking tape. Either a hand-cut or manufactured stencil can be used. Use a dry brush with a swirling or stippling technique to apply the stencil paint.

2 Apply the paint with a brush, drawing it off in one direction. It covers very well and dries rapidly to create a slightly rough texture. Apply second or third coats as required.

4 Since stencil paint dries almost instantly, you can blend in further colors to provide subtle shading. Protect the surface with varnish to prevent marking while handling.

Gilded
Picture
Frame

❖

A picture frame, whether it is old or new,
may be easily transformed into a fabulous
gilded antique frame by using gilding
creams. Traditional gold leaf is both
expensive and requires considerable skill in
application, whereas gilding creams offer an
affordable but good quality alternative.

❖

You will need...
- Masking tape
- Red oxide primer
- Paintbrush
- Gilding creams
- Soft cloth
- Mineral spirits
- Steel wool
- Gilding varnish (optional)

1 Protect the glass surface of the picture frame with masking tape. Apply a coat of red oxide primer. Apply more coats as required.

2 Apply the gilding cream with a cloth. A single color may be used or a number of similar shades can be subtly blended together. Any excess gilding cream can be removed with mineral spirits.

3 Let the finished surface harden, preferably overnight, and distress the surface slightly by rubbing lightly with some steel wool. The dull red base is an ideal complement for the gilded surface.

4 Remove the masking tape and clean the edges. The finished result, although very durable, can be made even tougher with a coat of gilding varnish.

METAL

❖

The natural corrosion of some
metals is usually a very slow
process and often produces
spectacular effects such as
natural verdigris on copper or
brass. This natural process can
be imitated and speeded up by
treating new metal surfaces.
Metal surfaces also lend
themselves to a huge variety of
finishes such as enamel
painting, distressing or even
black leading, all of which have
their own distinct style
and character.

Verdigris
Candelabra

❖

Most metal surfaces become weathered and corrode over a period of time. On some surfaces, such as brass and copper, this is particularly attractive.

The appearance of old brass, with its smooth, well-worn luster and distinctive mottled green patches of verdigris can easily be reproduced on a shiny new candlestick with a variety of paints and some sandpaper.

❖

You will need…

- Mineral spirits
- Soft cloth
- Gray acrylic spray paint
- Paintbrushes
- Light green latex paint
- Viridian artist's watercolor
- Sandpaper or abrasive foam pad
- Raw umber acrylic paint

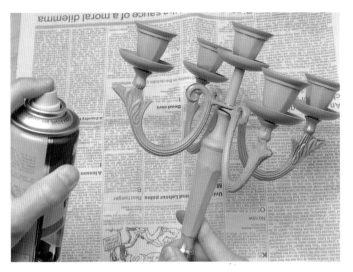

1 Wipe down the new brass with mineral spirits to remove any grease and dirt, then spray the whole candelabra with a thin, even coat of gray acrylic paint.

2 Mix light green latex paint with viridian watercolor paint to make a verdigris turquoise color. Brush over the gray base coat to create light and dark patches.

3 When dry, lightly rub the surface with sandpaper. Rub down to the brass on relief areas or parts that would be frequently handled. Reveal the gray base coat in some areas.

4 Finally, apply a very diluted wash of raw umber acrylic paint. This will stay in the crevices and tone down the newness of the green paint.

Gilt
Wall Lamp

❖

Although modern fixtures are often well designed, they are usually manufactured with relatively cheap materials. This gilt lamp is a typical example. An original lamp would be made of brass, which would need to be polished regularly to maintain its appearance, whereas this copy is finished with a thin layer of lacquered gilt. Frequently this top coat becomes damaged, leaving a tarnished appearance. You can take advantage of this by removing the top layer and deliberately tarnishing or patinating the surface. Try this technique also with door handles, knockers and other household fixtures.

❖

You will need…
- Paint remover/caustic soda solution
- Cloths
- Mineral spirits
- Tourmaline or metal patinating solution
- Cotton pads
- Jade oil

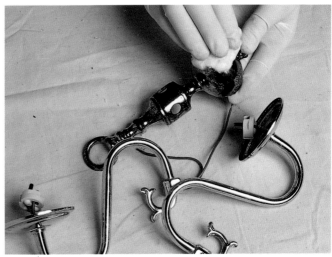

1 Remove the lacquer and gilt with a commercial paint remover or by dipping the fixture in a caustic solution. Always take care to protect or remove the wiring. Clean the surface with mineral spirits.

2 Gently pat the tourmaline, or metal patinating solution, against the surface with a cotton pad.

3 The patinating process is very rapid. Stop it when required by cleaning the surface with a damp cloth.

4 Fix the finished surface to prevent further discoloration by rubbing it with a little jade oil. When dry, this provides a tough and durable finish.

Restored
Edwardian
Fireplace

❖

It is always a good idea to have original
architectural fittings, such as a fireplace, to
fit the character and style of your home.
This Edwardian surround is typical of many
which were painted in the past. It needed to
be stripped before finishing with a natural
look of black lead.

❖

You will need…
- Paint remover
- Steel wool
- Rubber gloves
- Mineral spirits
- High-temperature flat black paint
- Soft cloth
- Black lead

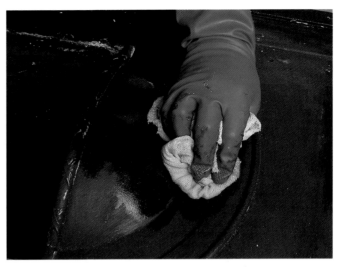

1 Take off the previously painted surface with a paint remover. It may require a number of applications. Use steel wool to remove paint from the molded areas.

2 When the paint has been removed, wash thoroughly with mineral spirits and steel wool.

3 Apply a coat of high-temperature flat black paint and leave to dry.

4 Use a soft cloth to add a coat of black lead. Then buff to a natural soft sheen.

Decoupaged
Watering
Can

❖

Decoupage became very popular during the Victorian period and was used to create intricate three-dimensional images on all kinds of household items. The decoupaged images that were used to decorate this old-fashioned-looking watering can are very simple farm animals, taken directly from a wallpaper border. The delicate cracked finish, known as craqueleure, has been achieved with a combination of oil- and water-based varnishes.

❖

You will need...
- Metal primer
- Paintbrushes
- Sandpaper
- Colored latex paint
- Acrylic- and oil-based varnish
- Decoupage scraps and scissors
- Craft glue solution
- Sponge
- Two-pack craqueleure (contains oil-based patina varnish and water-based gum arabic)
- Detergent
- Gilding cream or oil-based paint
- Mineral spirits

1 Paint the galvanized surface with a suitable metal primer. When thoroughly dry, rub with a fine grade sandpaper.

2 Apply a dark green latex paint and leave to dry. Second or even third coats may be required in order to obtain a good finish. Acrylic or oil-based eggshell paints can also be used.

3 Seal the base coat with acrylic- or oil-based varnish. Eggshell finishes may not require sealing, but they will require longer drying times.

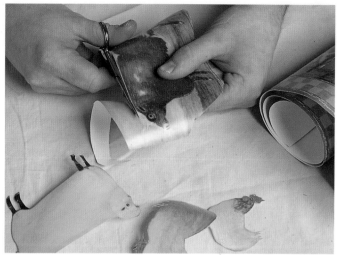

4 Select images to decorate the watering can: wrapping paper, borders and decoupage books are all good sources of designs. Cut out the images with sharp scissors.

5 Leave the images to soak in a dilute craft glue solution for a few minutes. Craft glue is ideal, as it dries to a completely clear finish.

6 Apply another coat of glue before carefully positioning the images. Use a damp sponge to remove any air bubbles which are trapped.

7 When the glue has dried, seal the surface with a coat of acrylic- or oil-based varnish. When the varnish has dried, apply a coat of oil-based patina varnish. Take care to apply an even coat.

8 When the surface feels almost dry, but slightly sticky, apply a coat of water-based gum arabic. If splitting occurs, mix a little gum arabic with detergent and reapply. Cracks will form as the two layers dry at different rates.

9 When dry, rub oil-based paint into the surface. A wax gilding cream is used here to give gold crackles. Remove any excess oil paint with mineral spirits.

10 When the oil-based paint has thoroughly dried, coat the surface with an oil-based varnish. This gives a very natural antiqued appearance.

Hand-painted Coffee Pot

❖ ◆

Traditional and simple hand-painting can be used to decorate almost any item and is frequently known as tole painting. You can decorate objects as large as a canal boat or as small as this enameled coffee pot. Designs can be traced or marked onto the surface to act as a guide and you can produce your own unique work of art in no time at all.

❖ ◆

You will need…
- Source designs
- Soft marker pencil
- Assorted colors of enamel or cold cure ceramic paint
- Assorted artist's brushes
- Palette or old plate

1 Original designs are widely available in source books and, if required, can be traced or copied onto the surface using a soft marker pencil. When the work is finished, simply rub these guidelines off.

2 Build up base colors, blending as required on a palette. Use a well-loaded brush and steady brush strokes to apply paint.

3 While the base is still wet, apply the highlighting color and let the two bleed together to create natural shading.

4 Simple detail, such as this painted design, helps to complete the item nicely but it could be accomplished with the use of a suitable stencil instead.

Painted
and Crackled
Coal Scuttle

❖

Items such as this coal scuttle have
frequently outlived their intended use and
are often discarded. They can, however, be
given a new lease on life as new household
items such as planters and wastebaskets.
The crackled finish imitates the natural
crackling that can occur on some painted
surfaces, letting it blend well with many
decorative schemes.

❖

You will need…
- Sandpaper
- Assorted water-based paints
- Paintbrushes
- Acrylic crackle medium
- Acrylic- or oil-based varnish
- Furniture wax and colorant

1 Thoroughly clean the surface, rub it down with sandpaper and prime with a suitable paint.

2 Apply a number of colors randomly to the surface. This creates the layer which will eventually show through the cracks, and can also be painted with a single plain color.

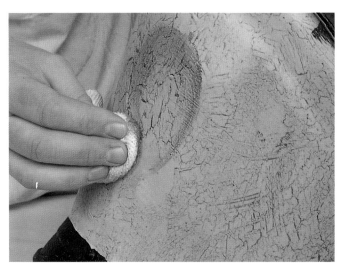

3 When dry, apply a coat of acrylic crackle medium to the whole surface. Then apply the top coat of latex or acrylic paint with a well-loaded brush. Keep rebrushing to a minimum, since it prevents crackling.

4 When crackling is complete, varnish the surface or rub with a little colored wax to tint it, then pick out the edges and inside of the scuttle in a complementary color. Decorate the surface as required.

Restored
1930s
Fireplace

❖

A fireplace is central to the character of a room and can provide the focal point and style on which to build. This 1930s fireplace was originally stove-enameled and has now been finished with hammered metal paint with a hint of gold. Similar finishes can be used on most surfaces and look particularly good on old cast-iron radiators.

❖

You will need...
- Paint scraper
- Sandpaper
- At least two colors of hammered finish paint
- Assorted brushes
- Oil-based gold paint
- Black eggshell paint

1 Scrape away the previously painted surface with a paint scraper. Rub the surface thoroughly with sandpaper to provide a good base for the hammered finish paint.

2 Apply the paints randomly and stipple two or more colors together to obtain the desired blend of colors.

3 While the hammered finish is still wet, stipple in a little oil-based gold paint and blend until the desired mix is achieved.

4 Once again, while the surface is wet, spatter some black eggshell paint over the surface by tapping a loaded brush against a firm surface. The resulting finish dries to provide an authentic look.

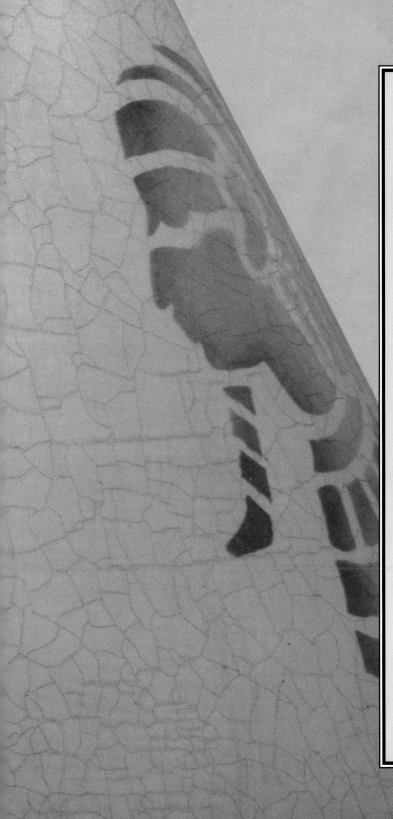

PAPER AND LEATHER

❖

Thousands of everyday household items are made from paper. With time, the sun will fade print and bleach color from paper, while continuous handling means that edges become damaged and creases become weak. All of these effects can be achieved in a fraction of the time using a variety of aging techniques. Leather is one of very few materials which actually improves with time. In general, you need a very specialized process to work and manufacture items in leather, but it is still relatively easy to age the surface and produce simple tooled effects.

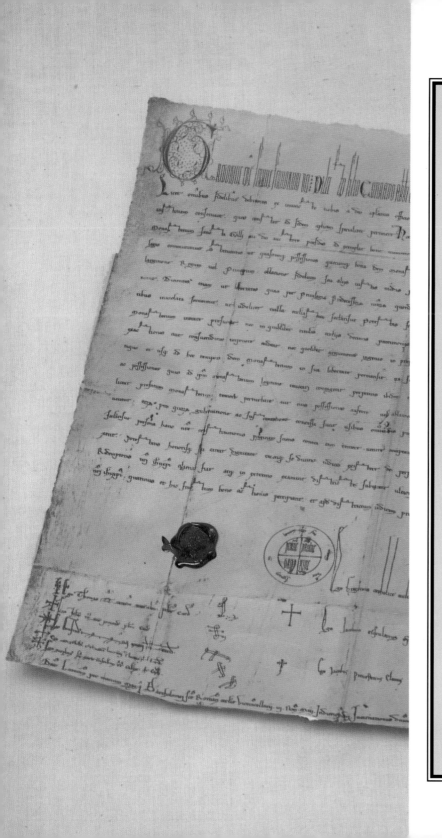

Aged Manuscript

❖

Ancient maps, illustrations and manuscripts can be fascinating and provide ideal wall decoration. Real manuscripts are, of course, both very rare and extremely valuable, but photocopies of originals can usually be obtained from larger libraries. Ordinary photocopiers will copy shades of color and reproduce them in shades of black on a plain white background. Color copying can also be used. This black and white copy is taken from an old text, written in Latin.

❖❖

You will need...
- Photocopy of original
- Strong cold tea
- Sealing wax
- Seal

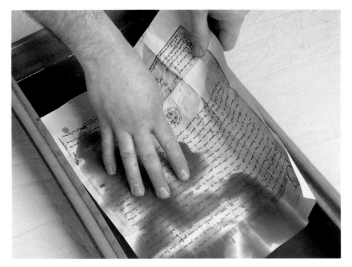

1 Fold and crease the paper. Soak in a strong cold tea solution to achieve a natural, aged color tint.

2 Rinse the paper and leave to dry. Trim the edges by tearing against a straight edge, rather than cutting the paper.

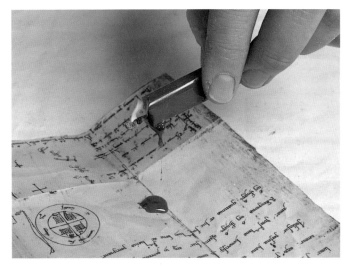

3 Drip sealing wax onto the surface to form a small pool. This wax can cause burns, so take special care during this operation.

4 While the wax is still molten, press the sealing dye into it. The sealing wax gives a wonderful authenticity to the document and can be personalized by using your own initials or family seal.

Aged Paper Lampshade

❖

It can be difficult to obtain lampshades which are both attractive and match your room and the lamp base. This decorated shade has been created from an off-the-shelf purchase and can be tailored to any decorative scheme. In this case, it resembles a shade from the 1930s when fascination with Egypt and the pharaohs was at its height.

❖

You will need...

- Acrylic varnish
- Assorted paintbrushes
- Template paper
- Polyester film
- Suitable stencil design
- Permanent fine-tip marker pen
- A sheet of glass
- Hot knife stencil cutter or craft knife
- Spray adhesive
- Masking tape
- Stencil paint
- Stencil brushes
- Palette or old plate
- Water-based crackle medium
- Artist's oil paint
- Mineral spirits
- Soft cloth

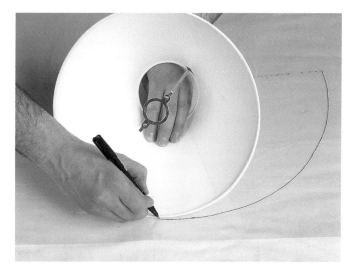

1 Seal the shade with acrylic varnish. Apply several coats and let the surface dry between each coat. Mark a template either directly onto the polyester or onto paper by rolling the shade and marking the top and bottom edges.

2 Take a suitable design from an available source book. You can use a photocopier to alter sizes if required. Trace the design onto the polyester film with a permanent fine-tip marker pen.

69

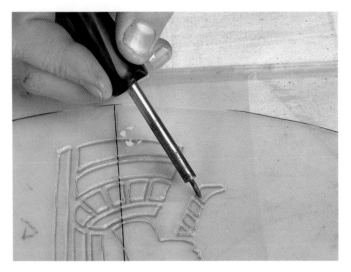

3 Place the design under a piece of glass. Line up the stencil template and use a hot knife stencil cutter to cut out the design.

4 Attach the stencil with a combination of spray adhesive and masking tape. Make sure the seam in the shade falls at the back.

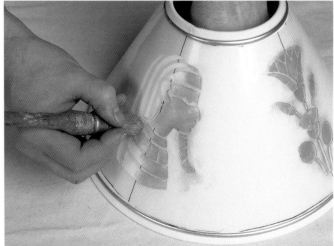

5 Work the paint well into the brush on an old plate or palette. Use tiny amounts of stencil paint to achieve the best results.

6 Apply the paint with either a stippling or swirling action. The paint will dry as it is applied, so a shading effect is achieved.

7 Apply second or even third colors immediately to give a more interesting and stylish effect. When the stencilling is complete, leave to dry thoroughly and apply another coat of acrylic varnish.

8 Apply a base coat of water-based craqueleure according to the manufacturer's directions.

9 When the base coat has dried, apply a top coat. Either fine or large-crack versions are available; here the large-crack version has been used. Leave the top coat to dry overnight.

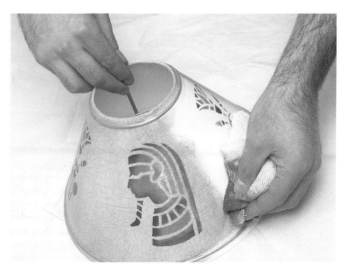

10 Use artist's oil paint to highlight the cracked surface and produce an impression of age. Remove excess oil paint with mineral spirits on a soft cloth. Protect with an additional coat of varnish.

Decoupaged
Picture
Frame

❖

Simple modern picture frames, or other items, can often be improved with the simplest of techniques. Gesso can be used, for example, to create molded and shaped ornaments to embellish surfaces before further decorating, such as gilding. This simple method shows how stylish and authentic results can be achieved with a minimum of effort.

❖

You will need…
- Cake trim or decoupage item
- Sandpaper
- Craft glue
- Furniture wax
- Artist's oil paint
- Soft cloth
- Mineral spirits

1 Cut the embossed gilt cake trim to fit this simple modern black frame. Alternatives such as embossed paper, doilies or mass-produced plastic moldings can also be used.

2 Rub the surface lightly with sandpaper to provide adhesion. Use a craft glue to glue the paper trim in place.

3 When the adhesive has dried, rub a mixture of furniture wax and a little artist's oil paint into the surface with a soft cloth. Red paint is an ideal complement to a gilded surface.

4 When the wax has hardened, buff the surface to a natural satin sheen with a soft clean cloth. If required, excess wax can be removed with mineral spirits.

Stencilled
Paper
Fan

❖

In bygone times, no lady would be seen
without a fan to cool her down gently.
These days, they are more likely to be used
as a lampshade, decorative ornament or
wall hanging. Original lace fans are now
almost impossible to find. You can create
an old-style fan using modern lace as a
stencil to make a delightful image on
a plain paper fan.

❖

You will need…
- Masking tape
- Piece of firm cardboard or wood
- Scissors
- Lace or alternative
- Spray paint

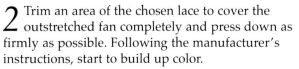

1 Stretch out the paper fan and tape onto a scrap of firm cardboard or wood. Mask out any areas you do not wish to spray.

2 Trim an area of the chosen lace to cover the outstretched fan completely and press down as firmly as possible. Following the manufacturer's instructions, start to build up color.

3 Continue to build up the depth of color. Use two or more different colors of paint if desired and then remove the lace. Leave the fan in place until it is thoroughly dry.

4 When the surface is dry, remove the masking tape and gently reform the shape of the original fan.

Leather Writing *Desk*

❖

Leather is widely used because it combines the two very desirable properties of flexibility and toughness. Obviously leather work can require specialist tools, equipment and considerable skill. However, this beautiful lap desk shows that it is possible to achieve great results with only the minimum of equipment.

❖

You will need...
- Red, dark green latex paint
- Vaseline
- Steel wool
- Acrylic- or oil-based varnish
- Cardboard
- Spoon
- Scissors
- Marker pen
- Heavy chain
- Leather and leather embossing tool
- Hot knife stencil cutter or soldering iron
- Mallet
- Antique leather dye or solvent-based wood dye
- Craft knife
- Clear leather polish
- Assorted paint brushes
- Rubber cement

1 Coat the lap desk with a base of dark green latex paint. Highlight areas which would normally undergo hard wear with some red latex paint.

2 Apply a little vaseline with your fingers. These areas will ultimately show up as distressed and should not be overdone or the end result may lose its realistic appearance.

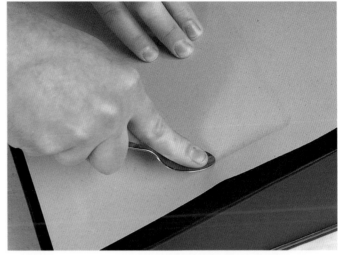

3 Apply dark green latex paint over the desk. When thoroughly dry, rub the surface vigorously with some steel wool. Areas previously covered with vaseline will have a distressed look. Protect the whole surface with varnish.

4 Mark a template to fit the insert by rubbing the back of a spoon over the positioned cardboard. When an embossed line is formed, carefully trim the cardboard.

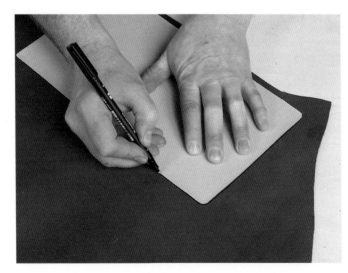

5 Use a permanent marker pen to mark the shape of the insert on the leather by drawing around the template. Then roughly trim the leather to shape with a pair of scissors.

6 Achieve an impression of normal use and age by beating the leather with a heavy chain. Protect the surface underneath and make sure the leather is on a firm base.

7 Mark a line an equal distance away from the template edge using a straight edge and hot knife stencil cutter or soldering iron.

8 Use a leather embossing tool and mallet to create an impression in the surface of the leather, taking care to work on a solid surface.

9 Rub the whole surface with an antique leather dye, according to the manufacturer's directions. A solvent-based wood dye may be used as an alternative.

10 Finally, trim the leather to shape with a sharp craft knife, polish with a little clear leather polish and set in place using rubber cement.

PLASTER AND STONE

❖

Plaster is a very versatile
material. A variety of good
molds are widely available if
you choose to make your own
casts. On the other hand,
finished plaster products are
often inexpensive and of very
good quality. Always wait until
the plaster has dried
thoroughly. Then the surface is
very durable and easy to paint.
As a material, stone gives the
impression of great strength
and permanence. Stone items
such as backyard ornaments
often improve with age as they
weather and become covered
with moss.

The aging process can be
imitated to produce a well-
established and mature look.

Powder Gilded *Cherubs*

❖

Finely ground metal powders and paint pigments are available in a wide range of colors. These can be blended and applied to almost any surface to produce excellent results. Small ornate plaster items, such as this cherub, can be cast, or bought ready-made. All fine powders, and particularly metals, should be used with great care.

❖

You will need…
- Red oxide primer
- Paintbrushes
- Craft glue
- Gilt powder
- Steel wool
- Oil-based varnish

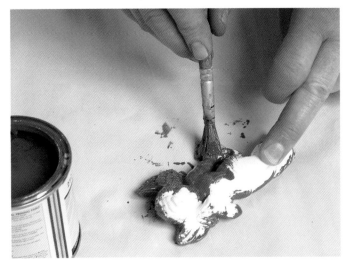

1 A newly cast plaster item should be left for at least one week to dry. When dry, apply a coat of red oxide paint. A second coat may be required to produce a good finish.

2 When dry, apply a thin coat of craft glue with a small brush. Be careful to avoid excessive buildup of glue in crevices since this will affect the quality of the end result.

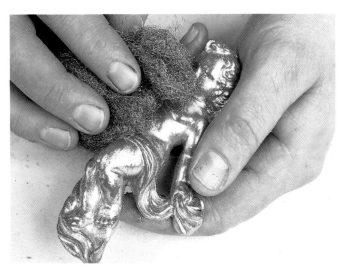

3 Pick up a little gilt powder on the end of a medium stiff brush and flick the brush toward the surface. As the gilding builds up, gently turn the cherub so that all surfaces are coated.

4 When dry, gently brush away any excess powder. Rub the surface lightly with some fine steel wool to expose a little of the dull red base. Apply a coat of oil-based varnish.

Marbled Plaster Bust

❖

Marble has a quality which has always been admired throughout the ages. The choice of colors and styles is enormous, as many factors affect the texture, pattern and faults created within the rock during its geological formation. When imitating marble, it is always useful to have either a real sample or photograph of the original. This plaster head is finished in a simple gray-marble effect to imitate a grand sculpture from an earlier age.

❖

You will need...
- Sandpaper
- Pale eggshell paint
- At least two tinted scumble glazes
- Assorted brushes
- Plastic bag
- Soft cloths
- Stencil brush
- Mineral spirits
- Fine artist's brush or feather
- Softening brush
- Oil-based varnish

1 Sand away any rough edges or burl marks on the plaster bust and apply at least three coats of pale cream or white eggshell paint.

2 Using a standard decorating brush, roughly apply two scumble glazes pretinted to your requirements. Either oil-based or acrylic water scumble glazes are suitable.

3 Blend the two glazes with a crumpled plastic bag. Concentrate on one color at a time, then gradually blend the two together. Dry the bag with a cloth to control the depth of color.

4 It is difficult to reach some areas with a bag. Use a stencil brush in these areas to blend the glazes. The surface should now have areas of shade subtly blended together.

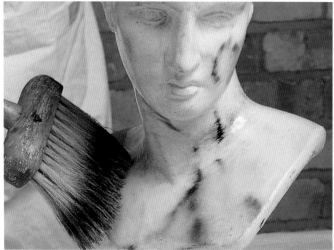

5 Mix artist's oil paint and mineral spirits together. Use a fine artist's brush or feather to paint the veins. Veins may branch and disappear, but shouldn't touch each other.

6 Blend the veins and background with a softening brush. Use a delicate pendulum action. Work first in the general direction of the veins, then at right angles to them.

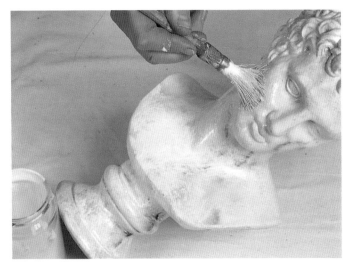

7 When the desired result has been achieved, leave the glaze to dry. Add more coats of glaze to help create the natural depth of color associated with natural marble.

8 Repeat the process of veining with a fine artist's brush or feather to add more detail. The marbled effect looks best if painted in layers.

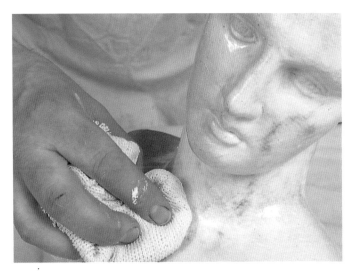

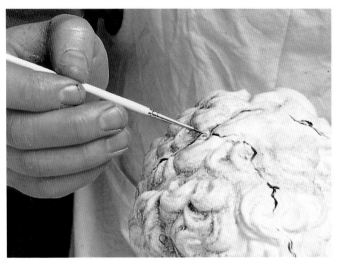

9 Stipple more coats of glaze with a cloth to create background depth.

10 When the finished glaze work has dried, protect the surface with varnish.

Ebony
and Ivory
Chess Set

❖

In past times decorative materials such as ebony and ivory were used for a wide range of items from piano keys to chess sets. However, the use of these materials today is now severely restricted for both cost and ecological reasons. However, very good imitations can easily be created without any damage to our pocketbook or the environment. This plaster cast chess set was ready made, but plaster casting sets are also available.

❖

You will need…
- Dark brown and pale cream eggshell paint
- Assorted paintbrushes
- Black and dark brown scumble glaze
- Soft cloth
- Acrylic varnish or furniture wax

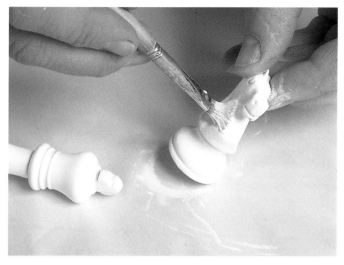

1 Apply the cream eggshell paint with a paintbrush. Apply second or even third coats to obtain a good surface.

2 A very dark brown eggshell is the ideal base for the ebony, which is traditionally thought of as black, but which is, in fact, a subtle mixture of dark brown and black tones.

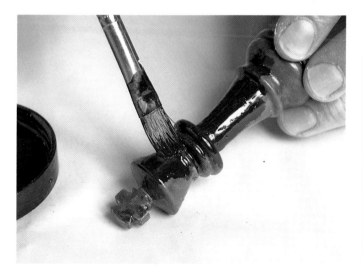

3 When the base has dried thoroughly, work a black scumble glaze over the surface, paying particular attention to the moldings. The glaze is slow-drying, so coat all the pieces before you proceed.

4 Dab the surface with a soft cloth, removing most of the glaze from the highlights but leaving the lowlights untouched. When the glaze has dried, protect the surface with varnish or furniture wax.

Aged
Concrete
Backyard
Ornament

❖

Any well-established backyard will contain
a host of decorative accessories which
complement the natural beauty of the
garden. The natural aging process for most
natural stone or terracotta is very lengthy.
The following technique will greatly
accelerate the aging process. This relatively
cheap modern trough is made from
concrete, but in only three weeks looks as if
it has been in the family for many
generations.

❖

You will need...
- Wire brush
- Paintbrush
- Live yogurt
- Cheesecloth

1 Remove any loose or flaky material by vigorously brushing the surface with a wire brush.

2 Brush the surface with a generous coat of live yogurt. Alternatively, bury the item in a mature compost heap.

3 Moisture and air are essential requirements, and by wrapping the surface with wet cheesecloth, both can be maintained. The surface should be kept damp, and, if possible, warm but not hot.

4 After only three weeks, the moss is developing well and will rapidly enhance the surface.

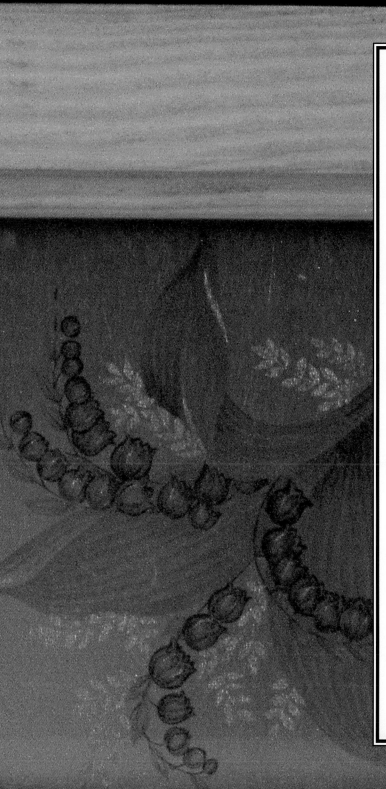

GLASS AND CERAMIC

❖

Although it is difficult to change the glass itself, the very fact that it is transparent means that a whole range of possibilities exist. It can be painted, etched or decoupaged to great effect, and you can even try making a mirror look old.

Ceramic surfaces are normally decorated with glazes and fired at the time of manufacture. This creates a very tough and durable surface that should change little with time. However, it is possible to copy ceramic antiques with today's cold-cure ceramic paints and resin sprays without needing to use an expensive kiln.

Aged
and Distressed
Mirror

❖

On old mirrors, the silver layer which
creates the reflective surface behind the
glass is protected only by a thin layer of
paint and is therefore vulnerable to damage,
which causes a slightly dull and often
imperfect reflection. This technique shows
you how to distress and age a new mirror.

❖

You will need…
- Paint remover
- Paintbrush
- Steel wool
- Mineral spirits
- Hematite or metal patinating solution
- Atomizing spray
- Black spray paint

1 Place the new mirror face down on a protected surface. Carefully brush on a coat of commercial paint remover. The surface will begin to blister and bubble. Reapply the paint remover as necessary.

2 When the base has softened, remove the protective layer by gently rubbing with steel wool, turning and changing it as required.

3 Clean the surface with a little mineral spirits and clean steel wool. When dry, spray a fine mist of hematite, or other metal patinating solution, onto the surface.

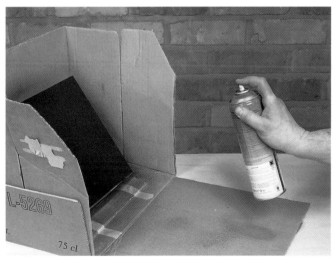

4 Metal patinating solutions act on the surface very quickly and should be washed off to prevent further discoloration. When dry, spray or paint the finished surface with an oil-based matte black finish.

Stencilled
Glass
Lampshade

❖

Glass and ceramic surfaces can be decorated
with hand-painted or stencilled designs to
make them look like antiques, or simply to
make them more attractive. Cold cure
ceramic paints, which don't require firing,
are available in a wide range of colors and
give excellent results. This etched glass
shade is ideal for a very simple but
effective design.

❖

You will need...
- Stencil design
- Piece of paper
- Stencil film
- Permanent fine-tip marker pen
- Scissors
- Sheet of glass
- Hot knife stencil cutter or craft knife
- Spray adhesive
- Masking tape
- Cold cure ceramic paint
- Stencil brush

1 Mark a template onto a piece of paper. Using the template as a guide, mark the stencil film with a permanent fine-tip marker pen. Cut the film with scissors.

2 Place the design under a sheet of glass and position the stencil film on top. Use a hot knife stencil cutter or craft knife to trace and cut out the image. Attach the stencil using spray adhesive. Use masking tape to attach the ends together.

3 Pick up a little cold cure ceramic paint with a stencil brush and work well into the bristle. Stipple the brush through the stencil, slowly building up the depth of color.

4 Leave the paint to dry for at least 3 hours. Carefully remove the stencil and leave the shade overnight to dry completely.

Decoupaged
Tissue Paper
on Glass

❖

Glass and ceramic surfaces can be decorated
with cold cure ceramic paints, although this
requires considerable skill. Fine designs can
often be found among decoupage scraps
and easily attached to the glass. However,
the transparency of the glass is lost, which
will affect the quality of the finished piece.
A simple napkin can be made to resemble
a hand-painted panel, as we have done
on this colorwashed display cabinet
to great effect.

❖

You will need…
- Printed tissue scraps
- Fine scissors
- Spray adhesive
- Matte varnish and brush

1 Remove the door to obtain a safe and convenient working surface. Clean and dry the glass thoroughly.

2 Trim the selected scraps with a pair of sharp scissors. Fine tissue paper can be difficult to trim and apply, so don't be over-ambitious.

3 Use spray adhesive to apply the tissue to the glass surface. Follow the manufacturer's directions.

4 Position the tissue paper carefully and smooth to prevent air bubbles from being trapped. If necessary, prick the tissue paper to release any trapped air. Apply several coats of matte varnish.

Mrs Brown's

VINEGAR

Malt Distilled

1 qrt.

Antiqued
Glass
Bottle

❖

Many old traditional kitchens were packed
with all kinds of homemade pickles,
preserves, and jellies with distinctive
handwitten labels. This simple glass bottle
has been authentically finished with
imitation etching and an aged label. A very
simple stencil has been used to achieve the
effect of acid-etched glass.

❖

You will need…
- Suitable stencil
- Spray adhesive
- Masking tape
- Oil-based stencil paint
- Stencil brush
- Palette or old plate
- Original artwork
- Scissors
- Solvent-based dark oak wood dye

1 Clean the glass surface and attach the stencil with
spray adhesive. Use masking tape to attach the edges.
Pick up a little paint on the tip of the stencil brush and
work it into the bristle on a plate or palette. Gently
stipple the brush through the stencil.

2 Create your own label by cutting and pasting several
designs. Photocopy to make several copies. Dampen
with a little solvent-based dark oak wood dye to color the
paper. When dry, glue into place with spray adhesive.

Spray
Crackled Lamp
Base

❖

You can create natural paint crackle finishes in a number of ways, but this spray-on crackle is widely available, easy to use, and very effective. Any ceramic surface which is either new but plain, or one which has perhaps been damaged and repaired, can be finished in this way.

❖

You will need…
- Spray box
- Spray crackle medium
- Acrylic paint
- Paintbrush
- Acrylic- or oil-based varnish

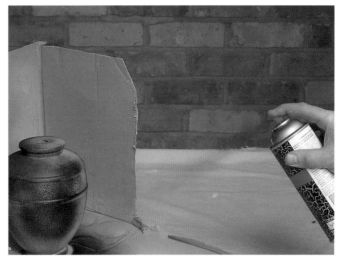

1 Make a spray box by cutting down two edges of a cardboard box. Protect the surrounding areas from spray fallout and spray the lamp base. Follow the manufacturer's directions, taking care to spray the paint evenly.

2 Apply the second coat after the recommended time has elapsed, once again taking reasonable care to spray evenly.

3 Crackling starts to occur immediately and will continue to develop as the top coat dries. The nature and style of cracks is controlled by the evenness and thickness of coats.

4 When the surface has thoroughly dried, decorate it further by hand painting or stencilling designs. Protect the surface with varnish.

Stamped Ceramic Tile

❖

Ceramic surfaces are usually decorated with hard-wearing glazes that are fused and hardened in a kiln at very high temperatures. This is obviously impractical for most individuals but, fortunately, the development of very hard-wearing resin paints, usually known as cold cure ceramic paints, means that a wide range of projects can now be tackled. This tile tea pot stand is decorated with a rubber stamp to create a pleasant hand-painted look.

❖

You will need...
- Cold cure ceramic paint
- Rubber stamp
- Assorted brushes
- Foam sponge
- Mineral spirits

1 Apply a small amount of paint to the rubber stamp using a brush or foam sponge. Apply the stamp to the surface with care to avoid smudge marks. Steady pressure and an even application of paint will ensure good results.

2 Gently lift away the stamp to reveal the impression. Add the border lines with a fine brush. Ceramic paint can take up to a week to harden completely. When thoroughly dry, insert the tile in its surround.

PLASTIC

❖

Today the range and versatility of plastic is enormous, and it can be used for almost any purpose. The very fact that plastic can be molded into any shape means that it lends itself to a wide variety of possible transformations, creating modern-day antiques from objects which would otherwise be very ordinary.

Verdigris
Frame

❖

The natural corrosion of most metals
containing copper produces a very
distinctive blue-green patina known as
verdigris. You can imitate this effect on most
surfaces with paints and glazes. Using this
method on this gilded plastic frame,
which has started to peel and look messy,
quickly transforms it into a stylish and
authentic fitting.

❖

You will need…
- Assorted water-based paints
- Palette or old plate
- Acrylic scumble glaze
- Stencil
- Paintbrushes
- Soft cloth
- Matte varnish (optional)

1 Tint the transparent scumble glaze prior to use. However, for items where exact color reproduction is not required, simply work from a palette or plate with a mixture of colors, glaze and solvent.

2 Using a small stippling or stencil brush, mix glaze and paint, and roughly work onto the ornate surface. Use a brush for each color and overlap colors as you apply them.

3 When the surface is covered, use a soft cloth to remove glaze from some areas and blend the colors so that no boundaries are obvious. Apply more coats of glaze when the base is dry.

4 The finished surface is reasonably durable, but can be protected with an appropriate varnish if required. A matte varnish will give the most authentic appearance.

Lacquered
Plastic
Bowl

❖

Traditional black lacquer work is usually associated with ancient Chinese or Japanese civilizations. Although most work was originally completed on either wood or papier-mâché bases, there is no reason today why any suitable base can't be used. This plastic bowl has seen its best days and much of the decoration has been worn away. However, it still has a nice shape and lends itself to restoration and redecoration as an imitation traditional Japanese bowl with gilded carp decoration.

❖

You will need…
- Fine sandpaper
- Flat black spray paint
- Cardboard box
- Suitable stencil
- Spray adhesive
- Masking tape
- Red and gold water-based stencil paints
- Stencil brushes
- Gilding cream
- Soft cloth
- Gold marker pen
- Satin or oil-based spray varnish

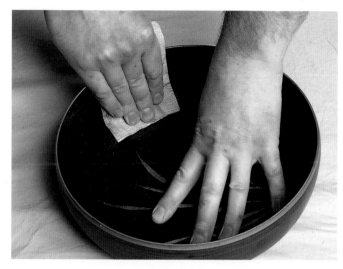

1 Rub down the base thoroughly with sandpaper to provide a good key for the spray paint, and also to remove any texture or design still remaining on the surface.

2 Use a cardboard box to make an improvised spray booth to help prevent excess fallout from spraying. Follow the manufacturer's directions to obtain a good finish.

3 This hand-cut stencil is taken from a specialist design source book, but ready cut stencils are also widely available. Use spray adhesive or masking tape to stick the stencil in place.

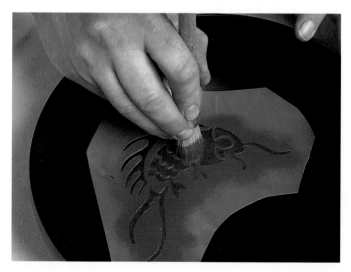

4 Pick up a small amount of crimson red stencil paint, work it into the brush and swirl the nearly dry brush through the stencil. The paint will dry quickly.

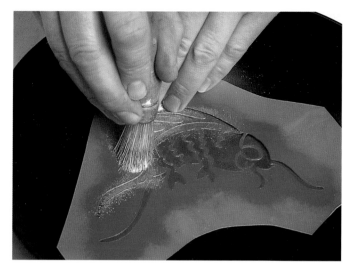

5 Use a gold stencil paint as a contrast with the crimson red; it can be added immediately. If the same brush is used, it should be washed and thoroughly dried between colors.

6 Remove the stencil immediately. Use masking tape to form a border around the top of the bowl. Use the crimson red stencil paint and brush with a stippling action to create an eye-catching border around the top edge.

7 Apply a little gilding cream with a soft cloth or dry brush to create a beautiful gold rim.

8 Use hand painting with brushes or a gold marker pen to enhance a design and provide detail, which would otherwise require multi-layer stencils. Protect the finished bowl with the spray varnish.

Aged Plastic Urn

❖

Plastic garden ornaments have significant advantages over traditional terracotta or stone since they are frostproof, more or less unbreakable and usually less expensive. However, despite significant improvements over the years, they still look like plastic and don't change with time in the same way that natural materials do. This technique provides a surface which will weather naturally and look far more attractive.

❖

You will need…
- Sandpaper or sharp blade
- Craft glue
- Paintbrushes
- Assorted grades of dry sand

1 The manufacturing process for molded plastic products often means that joints and edges have rough burl marks. Remove these by using the edge of a sharp blade or sandpaper.

2 Brush a coat of craft glue onto the surface. If necessary, leave the first coat to dry and apply a second.

3 Sprinkle a fine grain silver sand over the surface, taking care that all faces are covered. When the glue has thoroughly dried, rub the surface lightly with a soft brush.

4 For a coarse finish, recoat the surface with glue and once again sprinkle with a gritty sand. When dry, this is weatherproof but may be artificially weathered using the technique outlined on pages 90-91.

COMPOSITION BOARD

❖

One of the most useful manufacturing materials for decorative accessories is composition board. It can be machined and worked like wood, but it does not warp, bend, twist or shrink. Because it has no grain, it behaves the same way in all directions and is ideal for painting. However, take care when working with composition board, since the dust created is toxic and should not be inhaled.

Tortoiseshell Umbrella *Stand*

❖

Tortoiseshell was frequently used by the Victorians to decorate a whole range of household items. It is possible to achieve a realistic copy by using only paints and varnishes. Larger pieces of furniture can also be treated with this striking finish. Here, a natural red base color is used, but a strong yellow is just as attractive.

❖

You will need...
- Sandpaper
- Bright red and black eggshell paint
- Paintbrushes
- Dark oak stain varnish
- Black and burnt umber artist's oil paint
- Softening brush

1 Paint the sanded and cleaned composition board base with a bright poppy-red eggshell paint. When dry, repeat the whole process until a good surface is achieved. Apply a coat of dark oak stain varnish.

2 While the varnish is still wet, apply dots of black artist's oil paint in a regular pattern. Over each dot, paint a "V" or top hat with burnt umber artist's oil paint.

3 Using a softening brush, blend the colors, first in one direction, and then at right angles, until the desired look is achieved.

4 When this base has dried, sand it as required and apply several coats of the stained varnish. Pick out the moldings with black eggshell paint to provide the finishing touch.

Stencilled and Glazed *Wastebasket*

❖

The natural aging processes can be imitated by using glazes to provide background color and shading, and craqueleure to imitate the crackling which frequently occurs with old varnishes and lacquers. In this case we have recreated the effects of perhaps a hundred years or more in less than one week. The techniques can easily be adapted to good effect on almost any surface.

❖

You will need...

- Sandpaper
- Eggshell paint
- Paintbrushes
- Transparent scumble glaze and colorant
- Stippling brush
- Artist's oil paint
- Soft cloth
- Stencil
- Spray adhesive/masking tape
- Stencil paints and brushes
- Acrylic- or oil-based varnish
- Two-pack craqueleure
(contains oil-based patina varnish and water-based gum arabic)
- Mineral spirits

1 Rub the surface down with sandpaper, then clean and coat with an eggshell paint. When dry, repeat the process until a good surface is achieved.

2 Mix and brush small quantities of two glazes onto the surface. We have used transparent oil glaze tinted with artist's oil paint here, but acrylic scumble glaze is equally suitable.

3 Gently stipple each area in turn, and then blend the colors by stippling between the two. Clean the brush as required by rubbing on a clean absorbent cloth.

4 When the surface has thoroughly dried, attach your stencil in place with spray adhesive or a little masking tape, and work a small amount of stencil paint into the brush.

5 Apply the paint through the stencil using a swirling or stippling action. The paint will dry almost immediately, giving control over the depth of color.

6 Using this technique achieves a subtle blending of colors. Repeat the process until all faces have been completed. When dry, it is best to seal the surface with either acrylic- or oil-based varnish.

7 Craqueleure takes advantage of the different drying rates of oil- and water-based varnishes. Apply an even coat of oil-based patina varnish to the sealed surface and set aside to dry.

8 When dry, brush on the water-based gum arabic, and again leave to dry. If large cracks are required, force dry the surface with a hair drier. The shrinking top coat creates a crackled surface.

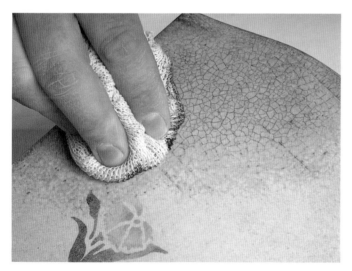

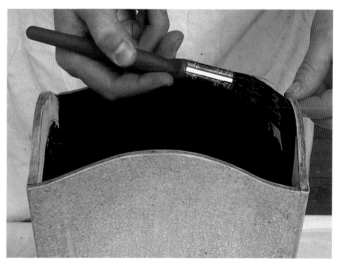

9 When thoroughly dry, highlight the crackles by rubbing them with artist's oil paint. Clean the surface with a soft cloth and a little mineral spirits.

10 When the oil paint has dried, protect the surface with an oil-based varnish to prevent the gum arabic from resoftening. Finish the interior of the basket with an olive green paint.

Decoupaged
Victorian
Firescreen

❖

The Victorians were fascinated by
decoupage and it was certainly at its height
of popularity in their era. They would
painstakingly cut out scraps of paper and
photographs, color them by hand, then glue
to a surface. Then they applied coat after
coat of varnish until a perfectly smooth
surface had been achieved. Today, printed
and even trimmed scraps are readily
available, and we have used them here to
create a typical Victorian screen.

❖

You will need…

- Black latex paint
- Paintbrush
- Decoupage scraps
- Fine scissors
- Craft glue
- Craft knife
- Acrylic- or oil-based varnish
- Fine sandpaper

1 Coat the firescreen with a black latex paint. Only the moldings will be visible, but it is useful to paint the whole surface, since this stops the glue from drying too quickly.

2 Carefully trim the decoupage scraps with sharp scissors. These printed sheets are partly trimmed to save time, but gift wrap or even photocopies are equally suitable.

3 Slightly dampen the paper to let it stretch, and attach to the surface with glue. The glue dries completely clear and can be brushed over the surface of the images. Continue to build up the pattern, overlapping images as you go.

4 When the adhesive has thoroughly dried, trim the edges with a craft knife. Protect the surface with a minimum of three coats of varnish, rubbing with fine sandpaper between coats.

INDEX

Technical Terms

This book contains a number of technical terms that may be unfamiliar to readers who have not tried a particular craft technique. Check with your supplier, who should be able to explain or help you find the materials you need.

There may also be words in the book that are unfamiliar to UK readers. The following list gives the UK equivalent for terms that may cause confusion.

US term	UK term
Cellophane tape	Sellotape
Composition board	MDF
Craft glue	PVA glue
Dark oak solvent stain	Dark oak spirit stain
Latex paint	Emulsion paint
Mineral spirits	White spirit
Muslin	Calico
Pickling wax	Liming wax
Rubber cement	Contact adhesive
Solvent-based wood dye	Spirit-based wood dye
Spray adhesive	Fixative
Steel wool	Wire wool

CREDITS

I would like to thank Quarto Publishing, and in particular Cathy Marriott and Toni Toma, for giving me the opportunity to create these projects. All the staff at The Painted Finish have also given invaluable help by taking on the extra workload and supplying virtually all the blanks, glazes, brushes, paints and inspiration. The vast experience of and help from Ian Howes is very much appreciated, and I look forward to working with him again. Most importantly, I would like to thank Paula, my wife, whose natural style and flair never cease to amaze me.